50 HABITS OF SUCCESSFUL YOUNG LEADERS

20 Daily Rituals Of Successful Leaders: Develop Admirable Leadership Strengths And Leadership Traits To Accelerate Your Career

DEREK SMITH

TABLE OF CONTENT

INTRODUCTION

The meaning of success is an emotional one. In any case, for a great number of people, it likely includes some degree of professional accomplishment, financial security with the goal that you can accommodate yourself and your family, and a group of individuals throughout your life who love you and are there for you. Unmistakably, these are things not every person has.

CHAPTER 1

Habits Of Successful Young Leaders

Successful young leaders know there is an opportunity to get better consistently in their leadership style. Regardless of whether you have simply been elevated to your first leadership position or you have been an executive for a considerable length of time, there are habits you need to learn consistently and approaches to follow so that you can turn out to be better.

To be a successful young leader, this is a list of habits you should learn;

1. EMULATE THE HABITS OF TODAY'S BEST LEADERS

One surefire approach to improve is to contemplate and copy the practices of today's best leaders. From building your listening abilities to being proactive, here are habits they especially esteem so you can put yourself on target to arriving at new statures expertly.

2. FACE CHALLENGES

An incredible young leader is bold yet reasonable. You ought to be prepared to confront difficulties and answer for the outcomes of your choices.

3. BE HONEST

Tell your colleagues regarding both great and awful news, and how the organization will respond. You are responsible for building up a quiet domain among your co-workers, so they are certain they are probably not going to be hit with bad surprises.

4. WIN TRUST

Your team will stay engaged and steadfast on the off chance that they believe they are encircled by individuals they can trust.

The first and most significant part of building trust is to engage in co-workers or representatives regular work issues. Give close consideration to the individuals who are behind every other person, and dedicate some an ideal opportunity to explaining their work to them.

The subsequent step is to be aware of their lives outside the workplace. Be that as it may, do not go too far, no one loves nosy supervisors.

5. RESIST THE URGE TO PANIC WHEN THING GO WRONG

Keep calm, successful leaders never show their feelings when they are angry. You need to remain focused, and in the event that you feel overpowered, it is smarter to go for a stroll or even remain and work from home.

Your associates, team mates, and even your directors commit errors; all things considered you can never permit yourself to address them out of resentment. Rather, serenely clarify the circumstance and the positive change you hope to see of them later on.

6. PURSUE YOUR PASSIONS

In spite of the fact that it is a piece old hat, the facts shows that you will never turn into a successful leader if you are going off course in your career. Being youthful permits us to attempt to comprehend what is fascinating yet valuable for us. Utilize your time well.

7. LISTEN AND OBSERVE

In the event that you are resolved to turn into a successful leader, you should be the best at listening and watching. Individuals communicate with their habits, words, and non-verbal communication consistently.

You can enlighten a great deal concerning an individual if you watch them. See what they are enthusiastic about, what makes them energized, which tasks make them miserable, and which appear to satisfy them.

8. SET AN EXAMPLE

Be simply the sort of leader you would follow yourself. You may not have the foggiest idea about each task 100 percent, yet it is basic to see how to illuminate or better improve every circumstance.

On the off chance that you were elevated to turn into a manager of a showcasing office, you need to know the details of the work and every worker there. It is you who must assume liability for each undertaking, and not your colleagues. Your primary point as a leader is to set a model; so for example, in the event that you need them to be on time with work schedule, you ought to be doing the same too.

9. BE ORGANIZED

Your work area ought to be clean and your requests ought to be straightforward. You should know the plan for every day and consistently.

10.   BE FAIR

Despite the fact that this is an undeniable proclamation, numerous leaders and administrators will in general pick their favorites. Regardless of whether you are a dear companion with somebody in your office, it does not give you the right to be absolutely lenient to them while tossing the greater part of the work to other people.

11.   WIN RESPECT

Winning respect is easy, all you need to do is act in a moral manner and model what you expect from the others in your group. Give them the idea that you know where you are going, and that you are guiding your group, and you are also doing the work with them.

12.   REMAIN CURIOUS

Millions saw the apple fall, yet just Newton inquired as to why. Interest is one of the principle characteristics of a decent successful leader. Remain enthusiastic, inquisitive, and focused on gaining some new useful knowledge.

13.   BE INNOVATIVE

What differentiates a leader from a follower?

Steve Jobs, one of the best visionary of our time responded to the inquiry above along these lines,

- Innovation differentiates a leader and a follower.

- In the quest to excel in this present relentless world, a leader must be innovative and creative simultaneously.

Incentive reasoning and steady innovation is the thing that makes you and your team stand out from every other person.

Thoroughly ponder out of the box to concoct remarkable ideas and transform those thoughts and objective into the real world.

14.   BE SYMPATHETIC

In spite of the fact that you must be tough, you ought to likewise comprehend that we are largely humans, and some of the time it will not hurt you to give a little leeway to those that are experiencing a harsh time, for example, an excruciating separation or loss of a family member.

15.   REMEMBER THAT YOU ARE YOUNG

You have some ideal opportunity to build a great career, and make sure to have a ton of fun and appreciate the second you are living in. While it is essential to be centered on your profession, your private life should not be affected.

16.   DO NOT PUT LABELS ON PEOPLE

In the event that you need to be a successful leader, you should lose the act of doling out names to other people and particularly to yourself. This incorporates the name of being a successful leader.

Who knows when your job might be repudiated, particularly in the event that you work for another person or in another company, or become smashed on the intensity of leadership? Your title isn't your character. Be sure, yet do not be certain in light of your name.

17.   UNDERSTAND YOURSELF

Attempt to do everything to see the influence you have on others. If you reach the stage that self-awareness is your quality, it implies you are all set on a long haul leadership venture.

18. LISTEN FIRST AND DECIDE LATER

Do not give in to the mindset that a successful leader exists absolutely to settle on significant choices.

A genuinely decent successful leader is somebody who tunes in to their group, urges them to impart their contemplations and insights, and settles on a choice in the wake of thinking about all viewpoints.

19. ENCOURAGE OPEN AND HONEST COMMUNICATION

To be an incredible leader, you must be an extraordinary communicator. Having transparent dialog imparts trust, assembles strong connections and guarantees those vital expectations remain on target. Also, bonds are reinforced and innovativeness is cultivated, which can prompt creative customer arrangements.

Open communication brings about individuals feeling esteemed and fortifies worker maintenance.

20. ORGANIZE AND FOCUS ON WHAT MATTERS

One propensity I live by is setting my needs from the get-go. I build up my greatest objective and afterward make a rundown of assignments required so as to achieve those objectives. By rehearsing this all through my profession, I have come to acknowledge what tasks matter and the ones that are basically time-squanderers. I have become progressively effective with my time, which benefits my group also.

21. KEEP UP YOUR COMPOSURE AT ALL TIMES

At the point when you can keep up your level-headedness regardless of what occurs, you will see that you are effectively affable. Numerous leaders will in general panic, and it typically unnerves or demotivates the group.

When you are ready to keep up a feeling of being cool, you can traverse your impediments with a breeze. Simply realize that each circumstance is not permanent and you will discover an answer for it.

22.   DELEGATE AND ELEVATE

A decent successful leader assigns the correct undertaking to the opportune individual and encourages them to thrive in that job.

Most successful leaders are worried about their own picture, yet incredible leaders give individuals under them significant tasks that will enable them to develop.

At the point when those under him see that the leader confides in them with significant tasks, they will get tied up with the vision and take the necessary steps for the association to flourish!

23.   FOLLOW YOUR INTUITION

Intuition is unpredictable and frequently requires quick judgment calls to be made in testing conditions, where you do not have the opportunity to reflect or set yourself up in advance.

In these conditions, I have seen instinct as the best leadership propensity, as it permits me to utilize my enthusiastic knowledge to locate the correct answer with an uncommon reputation of positive

results and great choices.

CHAPTER 2

Develop Admirable Leadership Strengths

24. LEAD YOUR TEAM LIKE A COACH

Each mentor knows the character of every one of his players. They realize who buckles down, who has outrage issues, who is consistently late and they realize how to function with them to get the best outcome. They take into account everyone in an unexpected way. I became acquainted with my group as people so I can inspire them, show them, and keep them close which results in a high performance in their various work.

25. CONTINUOUSLY FOLLOW UP IN WRITING

At whatever point you have a discussion, call or meeting with things to do, send a composed write up afterward with the things to do and who is responsible plainly stated. Things get lost or misjudged in communication. By sending an unmistakable development, you can take out those issues early and it will help guarantee you do not get shocked while looking into future expectations.

26.   SET ASIDE A FEW MINUTES FOR SELF-IMPROVEMENT

The one propensity that makes me a successful leader is steady personal development. I do this by reading books, going to meetings and through official training.

A few materials help me to remember what the most significant things are, some permit me to learn new apparatuses, and others assist me with distinguishing my vulnerable sides to develop in those zones.

27. HOLD REGULAR ONE-ON-ONE MEETINGS

I attempt to develop a solid relationship with every one of my workers. I focused on it to make sure I have a normal one-on-one session with every representative to check in and discover whether there is anything I can do to make their experience with me or with the team better.

It is likewise a space to share thoughts, which causes them to feel more and put resources into the organization, generally speaking.

28. BE VULNERABLE AND TRANSPARENT

As a leader, your greatest reward is trust and straightforwardness. Your group can peruse your feelings without any problem. For instance, as of late I began evaluating an alternate schedule that expects me to be inaccessible for three to four hours each morning. In our group meeting, I communicated to the group the reason and why taking that time was significant for me as well as for the business.

29.   EXPECT THE BEST IN OTHERS

At the point when somebody settles on an awful choice, it is easy to blame different people's judgment; however that is a terrible spot to begin. Rather, start by expecting the best in others. Perceive that a bad choice was likely made as a result of wrong data, not misguided thinking.

This methodology permits the other individual to conceal any hint of failure or is free from being shamed and blamed, and for the most part brings everything about them being undeniably progressively open to future proposals. They won't be scared of trying or doing their best next time.

30.   BE PROACTIVE

I like to prepare and be proactive about issues that may happen. Being proactive rather than responsive can assist you with feeling in charge and a stride on top of things consistently, which is so important in business.

31. REMAIN POSITIVE AND BRING OUT THE BEST IN YOUR TEAM

Put forth an attempt to draw out the best in others. Do what you can to persuade and rouse them. Show others how it is done. Your group needs somebody that lifts them up and encourages them to accomplish a significant task.

32. SPEAK LAST

I make it a point of duty to talk last when I am in a gathering comprising of employees I supervise. In addition to the fact that it is significant for me to process what every other person in the room needs to say, yet I need to ensure that my perspective doesn't predispose the thinking about everyone around me.

My objective is for the best thoughts and the best commitments from the colleagues to be developed, and to do as such, I avoid the interrupting them, speaking last is the best.

33.   SAY   YES   WHEN   AN OPPORTUNITY PRESENTS ITSELF

With the hustle and multifaceted nature of our everyday lives, it's not difficult to turn down opportunities in front of us hanging tight for the ideal fit or perfect planning. In any case, I have discovered that in both my expert profession and in my outside life, saying yes to circumstances has prompted progressively open entryways and a ton of extraordinary adventures.

Whenever you disapprove of chances, you are restricting yourself to the way that you are on and conceivably diminishing the potential for new development encounters.

While saying yes to each open door may not be sensible, try taking more risks and saying yes to all opportunities consistently, this can prompt unimaginable encounters and conceivable outcomes that you had never envisioned.

34. CONTINUOUSLY BE OPEN TO FEEDBACK AND ACTIVELY SEEK IT OUT

I attempt to ask or give a bit of useful criticism consistently. It places me in an outlook of consistent development and improvement, just as concentrating my brain on how I can help people around me develop and create.

I additionally make it a point to converse with at any rate one client daily. This causes me to remain near our client's needs and increase significant bits of knowledge with regards to how we can all the more likely serve them.

35.   KEEP IT POSITIVE AND STAY ADAPTABLE

Acing the specialty of catching negative contemplations and in a flash, saying, affirming and repeating positive thoughts multiple times in succession, and a couple of times for the duration of the day causes me to keep my head in a positive, imaginative mentality. In a similar vein, when faced with challenges, I have made instant acknowledgment training so I can adjust, alter, and execute to continue pushing ahead.

36. DISCOVER A HOBBY THAT KEEPS YOU COMPETITIVE AND IN SHAPE

I love work, and it would expend each waking moment of my life. In any case, I have discovered that I am better at my specific leadership work when I give my brain the space to learn new abilities and discover happiness in different daily issues.

Over the last decade, I have taken up planting, which I never would've set aside a few minutes for when I was 25.

I have adored being nearer to nature and our food framework, and the feeling of achievement to watch the nursery develop. It constrains me to back off and be tolerant, while giving me some little time to clear my brain for new thoughts.

Be certain to consistently spare your time for things that give you delight or things you adore, even on the craziest of work days. With stress and travel in the front line of a bustling leader's life, you need to spend a ton of deliberate exertion taking care of your wellbeing.

While I am continually shy of time and regularly in an alternate time region, I also practice tennis consistently with a lot more youthful and better players to challenge myself, regardless of the age difference. I likewise tried resolving to play serious tennis at the most elevated level conceivable in national level tennis competitions and local or neighborhood groups.

By focusing on this level, it drives me to prepare on and off the court however as much as I can. Also, it doesn't need to be tennis. I accept this applies to any serious game, outdoor activities or physical action.

CHAPTER 3

Leadership Traits To Accelerate Your Career

37.   DETACH FROM YOUR PHONE

A portion of my best thoughts work out as expected during my morning and night bike drives. During those occasions, I have the chance to not be diverted by work or performing various tasks. I feel free from work burden.

This lets my mind stream inventively and furthermore permits me to switch work setting and home life proficiently and all the more viably.

In case if you are not a bike lover, have a go at getting off your telephone when you're on the metro, or tuning to the radio while you're driving.

Simply let your inner mind think openly and see where it goes.

38.   DISCOVER A SYSTEM AND STICK WITH IT

I am exceptionally orderly. I imagine my ideal future. I set long haul objectives and build up a guide to achieve these objectives.

I depend on small scale objectives (90 days, 30 days, 7 days, and every day) to assist me with accomplishing my targets.

I am additionally an extremely standard arranged individual:

- Get up right on time

- get going (exercise)

- practice 10/10/ (10 minutes of reflection, 10 minutes of reading, and 10 minutes of journaling).

I attempt to boost 'my time' before the day dominates or starts fully.

My journaling exercise spins around appreciation (compelling me to think positive), my day by day vision and the three most significant goals I have to achieve that day.

I share this with a responsibility accomplice which is my wife, each morning. As far as I can tell, I'm bound to achieve a big work for the day on the off chance that I've resolved to do as such by being accountable to another person or imparting it to another person.

39.   GRASP CHANGE

The best business leaders can grasp change even when change is hard.

Steve Jobs had the option to build another generally successful computer organization in the wake of being approached to leave Apple.

Elon Musk had the option to create Tesla and SpaceX in the wake of leaving PayPal.

Cerebrum Chesky was eager to change Airbnb from a business centered on serving leaseholders to an overall housing stage.

Grasping change can make you an increasingly successful young leader.

As Jack Welch, the previous CEO of GE, stated, if the pace of progress outwardly surpasses the pace of progress within, the end is close.

40.   REMAIN CURRENT BY STUDYING THE LATEST TECHNOLOGIES

The pace of mechanical change will quicken once Artificial Learning (AI) and Machine learning (ML) package go standard.

The notable financial speculator Tomasz Tunguz predicts that AI and ML will change business as we probably are aware it.

For youthful business leaders to remain in front of the opposition, it is essential to create at any rate a simple comprehension of AI and ML so as to get ready for what's to come.

41.   PRACTICE   SERVANT LEADERSHIP

Servant leadership is the possibility that as a business leader you are answerable for engaging your group to progress as a matter of first importance.

As opposed to asking the individuals you lead to serve you and your objectives, instead you tutor and urge your group to hit their objectives.

Expecting that their objectives are lined up with the organization vision, the business will be successful when your group is effective.

42.   PRE-PAY YOURSELF INTO WIN-WIN SCENARIOS

I have created win-wins for various parts of my life, and I prepay them so I can't work myself out of them. For instance, I love investing energy with my spouse and we have to practice, so one win-win is that my better half and I train in Krav Maga together every Monday night.

We likewise utilize these night times as date evenings, paying our sitters well ahead of time so that, regardless of how worn out and irritable we may feel, we once in a while make the night a big hit. Which means, we get incredible exercise, a sentimental meal, and an opportunity to truly find one another and fortify our association each and every week? It's my preferred success win.

43.   COLOUR CODE YOUR CALENDAR

Consistently, endeavor to live in your fire and not in your wax. When you live in your fire, you are stimulated and energized. At the point when you live in your wax, you are doing things that are sapping your vitality. To observe between the two, I like shading coding (I mark it). I color code my schedule for all that I will do for the duration of the day.

I separate various capacities into different hues like;

- Light blue for calls.

- Dull blue for up close and personal gatherings.

- Orange for movement.

- Red is awful, for the most part saved for conversations with lawyers.

- Different shades of green are the things I do that are in my fire, such as composing, talking, and meetings.

Every day when I open my schedule I realize what sort of day I have. This empowers me to ensure that I plan my days to consistently have the opportunity to work in my fire.

A green day demonstrates I'm living in my fire and making the progress I need.

44.   MAKE TIME TO PEOPLE WATCH

This may sound odd, yet three to four times each week I take 30 minutes to sit and watch people. Human drawing with regular day to day existence, as basic as the attire they wear, to how they connect with innovation.

I likewise watch enthusiastic responses; like bliss and dissatisfaction. I'm lonely at the point at which I choose to have a perception hour and I take in something from it inevitably.

The minutes I spent watching individuals help me make an interpretation of what I see into my work, from another wind in a story I'm composing or a progressively natural structure for an iPhone application.

Since the world is changing so rapidly and individuals are diverted by the movement of regular daily existence, this standard of perception encourages me to stop for some time, however frequently opens my eyes to increasingly imaginative approaches to make. Being inspired by human existence can produce great innovative ideas.

45.   QUIT THINKING ABOUT WORK

Pondering about work day in and day out won't assist you with completing more. Actually, it will accomplish less. It's debilitating and leaves you feeling dead. It's imperative to discover another thing to concentrate your mind on outside of your profession.

Mine is music. I play console in a musical crew. It's an extraordinary method to loosen up and it permits my mind to work through all the everyday difficulties. It's a very amazing approach to clear all the messiness and keep me focused.

46. RELINQUISH BEING A PERFECTIONIST AND BECOME A PROGRESSIONIST

In the event that you believe the best way to be successful is to be 100-percent ideal; 100 percent of the time, you will wear out. It almost transpired with me. I used to be a perfectionist who concentrated on any easily overlooked detail that turned out badly versus commending everything that went right. I use to see the bad sides more than the good sides, this is very wrong.

Stop being a perfectionist, be a progressionist instead - somebody who commends their advancement consistently. In the event that you are close to an objective or complying with a time constraint, it is better to look how much further you need to go or commend how far you have come. At the point when I praise the advancement I make, it discharges endorphins and gets me re-energized to continue onward.

47.   QUIT OVERREACTING TO YOUR METRICS

I was lucky to learn right off the bat in my vocation the estimation of not overcompensating to each adjustment in a business metric. In my own business, those measures incorporate blog traffic, online course enrollments, and book deals.

We may understand that two pieces of information are not a pattern, they are not the same;

however I've likewise taken in some useful techniques that remind me regularly to make an effort not to clarify each highs and lows in a business metric.

The days will not always be good, in some days, we can acquire losses and some days, we can have profits. It's human instinct to respond, however that steady response and trying to clarify the situation can make individuals tired and it really diverts us from working well.

It also meddles with our endeavors to improve execution and discourages us from doing better next time.

A technique called process behavior charts envisions measurements and gives some factual guard rails that assist us with knowing whether a measurement is simply fluctuating or if it's changed in such a way that enhance understanding.

48.   EXPRESS YES TO STRESS

In the event that you can comprehend your pressure and decide your degree of capability in managing difficulties throughout everyday life, you will be prepared to confront troubles head-on with the aim of winning, which is far not the same as frightfully keeping away from life's difficulties and emergencies.

Search for triggers and have a plan set up for guaranteeing your achievement in any circumstance. Permit yourself to associate with your motivation, adjust designs appropriately, and in this manner set yourself up for considerably more achievement.

49. BREAK OR CHANGE YOUR HABITS

A great deal of my success depends on maintaining a strategic distance from worrying or being bothered. Consider a similar feast, a similar exercise schedule, a similar course to work. While they may function admirably, they become exhausting and that can execute innovativeness.

To remain a stride ahead, I put forth an intentional attempt to give something new a shot, a customary premise.

Indeed, even an apparently little change in one field, for example, attempting culinary practice or working with another foundation, can touch off a discovery in another piece of my life.

Focusing on re-evaluation will prepare you to surrender inflexible idea examples and face risk. Reward included, your gathering of contacts turns out to be increasingly differing in light of the fact that you have wandered out into a new area. Generally significant, re-evaluation keeps the excursion fun.

50. ENSURE THAT BEING SUCCESSFUL IS NOT HOW YOU MEASURE YOUR SELF-WORTH

At the stage when I turned into a dad, I was simply getting my organization off the ground. Obviously, I was eager to become hopelessly enamored with this fresh new little individual in my life, however I was likewise concerned: If my organization at any point got footing, would I say I would be constrained into a type of Faustian deal, exchanging my business against my family?

Thinking back on things up until now, I had everything incorrectly.

To be a successful business person, I required something outside of the workplace to turn into the center of my character. Honestly, this shouldn't be kids, or even family.

The only thing that is important is ensuring your feeling of self-esteem is attached to something decoupled from your success. In the event that success is the thing that you have to get to like yourself, then, you'll be hesitant or feel deplorable pressure when it comes to working and you will probably go through significant dangers.

Furthermore, incidentally, that will simply hinder your success.

Honestly, my recommendation is not to proceed to have a child before beginning an organization, just ensure that the center of your personallity and your feeling of self-esteem is attached to something more rigid than your organization's valuation.

Amusingly, this is simply the most ideal approach to set up for the hazard-taking you will encounter.

CHAPTER 4

DAILY RITUALS OF SUCCESSFUL PEOPLE

1) OWN YOUR CALENDAR

Invest heavily in first planning the activities that are the most important in your own life, not simply your expert life, offsetting noteworthiness with progress. On the off chance that you plan a morning run or an innovation free supper with your family, recall that it's similarly as critical to keep these arrangements as you would keep a meeting with the president.

2) RISE EARLY AND EXERCISE

Three years back, I made a guarantee to myself to begin my day with exercise and it has delivered unanticipated profits in body, brain and soul. Beginning your day with a standard wake up time and exercise routine assists with resetting from the earlier day and stimulate for the day ahead.

I regularly set my alert for 5:40 a.m. to give me simply sufficient opportunity to sit in the calm of my family room getting a charge out of some espresso and to prepare for a morning action to get my body going.

I attempt to change things up between a 2.5-mile walk, 45 minutes of yoga at home or an hour at the gym.

I feel better genuinely; however I am additionally ready to utilize an opportunity to reflect and process the highs and lows from the day preceding and meet the new day with a feeling of clearness and readiness for the chances and difficulties that lie ahead.

This day by day schedule is something I honor as an approach to remain on target and spurred.

3) SET ASIDE EFFORT TO BE INTROSPECTIVE AND JOURNAL

It's very liberating toward the finish of a taxing day to set aside the effort to process by means of journaling. I pen down the significant things that happened that day - what things disappointed me, things that I need to allude back to during a stormy day (like an incredible bit of input), concerns and objectives.

This training has helped me calm my thoughts, but at the same time it's empowered me to work out numerous barricades, regardless of whether it's identified with something occurring at work or self-improvement. In the event that you choose to journal, it's essential to truly be straightforward with yourself.

4) HAVE A CONSISTENT MORNING ROUTINE

For a considerable length of time, I have gotten up simultaneously, consistently, had a similar breakfast, and showed up at the workplace at generally a similar time. I hold a speedy daytime meeting with my group, set my plan for the day, and give myself some an ideal opportunity to complete stuff first, when I am refreshed and able.

5) START THE DAY WITH MEDITATION

I start each day with a short meditation and a run (ideally not on a treadmill). Making this responsibility encourages me to start every morning with a fresh start, recalling who I am and why I do what I do.

This tranquil reflection permits me to ground myself from disorder and commotion, making the entire day essentially increasingly beneficial, and giving motivation to accomplish my best work by concentrating on the way that I am serving individuals consistently.

6) ACE THE ART OF MICRO-ENJOYING MOMENTS

I used to hold up until the ideal chance to unwind and appreciate fun exercises, loved ones until I understood that there is no ideal time. Regardless of whether at work or in close to home life, you are continually going to confront difficulties and deterrents that can be difficult to place in a notorious lockbox.

While stress can be something to be thankful for that pushes you to be a successful work leader or more grounded person, I have discovered that you additionally need to build up the capacity to remain at the time. Consistently, I attempt to discover little, 15-minute squares to concentrate on happy things.

This could mean going for a stroll to the neighborhood café, getting the telephone (avoid the content) and calling a friend or tuning in to a digital broadcast.

Rehearsing the workmanship of miniaturized scale getting a charge out of life has helped me better face life's anxieties and position the main things into a point of view.

7) FOCUS ON A MORNING ROUTINE WHICH DOESN'T INVOLVE YOUR PHONE

It's enticing to promptly jump on your telephone and browse your email the second you wake up, particularly when you're running a startup. Indeed, I did that a lot even in the beginning phases of my business.

I made a promise to myself to begin my day by accomplishing something that encourages me to unwind, reset and position me to prevail or conquer in my day. Regardless of whether that is a five-mile run or a five-minute reflection, committing time to those exercises that cause you to feel great outside of work will make your time in the workplace considerably more satisfying and gainful.

8) ORGANIZE YOUR DAY IN CATEGORIES

The typical daily agenda routine can get overpowering, especially when the rundown begins to traverse numerous pages. Sorting your daily agenda into three distinctive prioritization levels, for example,

- must do today

- if time permits and

- can hold on for tomorrow

The prioritization levels permits you to see through the messiness of your everyday rundown and spotlight on the things that issue most, regardless of whether it's beverages with a partner or finishing an introduction for financial manager.

9) PRACTICE GRATITUDE AND READ (A LOT)

I have generally believed that having a point of view is basic to with self-awareness, so I put forth an everyday attempt to help it and grow it. To help it, I reveal to myself something that I am appreciative for at any rate once per day.

I find that this keeps me grounded and associated with the things generally significant in my life, yet additionally frequently gives a great point of view during testing or upsetting minutes in my day.

To extend my viewpoint, I read ... a great deal. Not really just books, yet everything from articles on recent developments to long peruse that bring a profound plunge into the most recondite issue.

Whether or not what I'm reading is identified with what I accomplish for work, I find that driving myself to see things contrastingly and trains my mind and at last empowers me to be progressively imaginative and successful in delivering plans.

10) THINK BEYOND PRACTICAL BOUNDARIES (DREAM BIG), BUT REALIZE ENTREPRENEURSHIP IS A BATTLE OF THE MIND

Eventually, your brain - not the cash is the thing that will separate you. We laud the hustle and imagine it's enjoyable to work 18-hour days. Wake up at the point when your body is shouting at you to back off, don't disregard it. Remain consistent with yourself and put your psychological well-being first. Achievement will definitely follow.

11)　DISAPPROVE OF MEETINGS

I refuse accepting any gathering invite that does not clarify what the target of the gathering is and why I am required. Time is cash may be an abused maxim, yet it's fantastically simple to become over-booked, and in the event that I spend my whole day in gatherings, I have brief period to dedicate to my own errands and needs.

12) BUILD A NETWORK OF SUCCESSFUL PEOPLE

Assemble a system by joining a functioning association, and make your essence felt by making an outsized commitment to the purpose.

In time, most of the individuals in the association will pay heed to you or notice you, and you will have the option to make significant business associations that will serve your thriving profession.

13) CONTINUALLY EDUCATE YOURSELF TO MASTER YOUR BUSINESS

The business world is evolving rapidly, and the pace of progress will keep on quickening with new innovation like machine learning and AI, among different advancements. For youthful successful leaders to remain on top of things, it is significant that you continually teach yourself.

Self-learning can come in numerous structures. There are various phenomenal online businesses and initiative courses offered by associations like Coursera and Khan Academy.

Going to live meetings about a particular field of business can likewise be useful, both in learning new accepted procedures and building a system.

14) LISTEN MORE THAN YOU TALK

You ought to listen more than you talk. Compelling authority requires understanding the thoughts, sentiments and necessities of your group. In view of this information, successful leaders should take conclusive and educated choices.

In any case, neglecting to tune in to associates or individuals in your group can produce disappointments and lead to helpless business results.

15) SPEAK WITH NONVERBAL CUES

A basic part of compelling initiative is having the option to convey viably. So as to do that, make sure to focus on significant nonverbal signals. Abstain from slumping, look and present a sure and quiet appearance.

16) EMBRACE CLEAR TASK MANAGEMENT GUIDELINES

For a youthful business leader, it can feel like the measure of work that should be done is ceaseless. To assist you with the remaining sorted out, it is imperative to build up an authoritative structure that makes it simple to organize work.

Receiving the Eisenhower choice, which shows the overall significance of the current issues, can be an incredible path for youthful leaders to figure out what ought to be done straightaway.

17) BE HUMBLE

As indicated by an investigation referenced in the Harvard Business Review, humble leaders will in general be progressively successful. The article characterizes a modest leader as somebody who can precisely get to their qualities and shortcomings without having a feeling of pride or ego.

Also, workers and colleagues will come to regard your sentiments all the more promptly in the event that they trust you can build up a supposition without letting sense of self-esteem disrupt everything.

18) GIVE AND ASK FOR CANDID FEEDBACK

Giving real criticism can be awkward from the outset; however the best associations and leaders can request input so as to lift up everybody included.

To make a culture that empowers genuine criticism, start by requesting it from associates and colleagues. When you set a genuine model, others will start requesting criticism too.

19) DISCOVER A WORKLIFE BALANCE

Setting aside work for yourself has been proven to improve efficiency and satisfaction.

While turning into a successful leader will require a lot of work well beyond the conventional 9-to-5 employment, it is as yet critical to discover time for yourself.

A viable method to make work life balance is to plan both work and individual exercises on a similar schedule. In the event that you are principled about ensuring your time, you will have the option to carry on with a decent and beneficial life.

20) LET LONG-TERM GOALS GUIDE DECISION MAKING

It is simple to give up to the day. Email, meetings and earnest works can make it hard to concentrate on significant long haul objectives.

However, it is significant that, as a youthful leader, you keep up a ground breaking viewpoint that organizes key attributes, thoroughly considering everyday work.

CONCLUSION

Successful youthful leaders can shape their reality and progress both in oneself and professionally. To turn into a successful youthful leader, consider receiving a portion of the key attributes exemplified by leaders like Steve Jobs, Elon Musk, Richard Branson and Brian Chesky.

As a youthful leader, it is imperative to figure out how to convey, organize and self-educate. This will engage you to oversee groups, and empower you to think deliberately today and lead effectively.

Toward the day's end, recall that you are youthful, with a great deal of time ahead. Buckle down, remain inquisitive, and recall that successful leaders don't disclose to you what to do rather they demonstrate how it's done.